Emotional Intelligence: Why It Can Matter more than any thing

A.HABIB

CHAPTER 1 : DEFINITION AND INTRODUCTION

Emotional intelligence has been defined, by Peter Salovey and John Mayer,as "the ability to monitor one's own and other people's emotions, to discriminate between different emotions and label them appropriately, and to use emotional information to guide thinking and behavior".

According to Daniel Goleman, an American psychologist who helped to popularize emotional intelligence, there are five key elements to it:

-Self-awareness.

-Self-regulation.

-Motivation.

-Empathy.

-Social skills.

Although the term first appeared in "The Communication of Emotional Meaning" paper by a member of Department of Psychology Teachers at College Columbia University Joel Robert Davitz and clinical professor of psychology in psychiatry Michael Beldochin 1964, it gained popularity in the 1995 book "Emotional Intelligence", written by author and science journalist Daniel Goleman Since this time, EI, and Goleman's 1995 analysis, have been criticized within the scientific community despite prolific reports of its usefulness in the popular press

Empathy is typically associated with Emotional Intellegence, because it relates to an individual connecting their personal experiences with those of others. However, several models exist that aim to measure levels of (empathy) EI. There are currently several models of emotion intelligence . Goleman's original model may now be considered a mixed model that combines what has since been modeled separately as ability EI and trait EI. Goleman defined EI as the array of skills and characteristics that drive leadership performance .The trait model was developed by Konstantinos V. Petrides in 2001. It "encompasses behavioral dispositions and self perceived abilities and is measured through self report ."The ability model, developed by Peter Salovey and John Mayer in 2004, focuses on the individual's ability to process emotional information and use it to navigate the social environment.

Studies have shown that people with high EI have greater mental health, job performance, and leadership skills although no causal relationships have been shown and such findings are likely to be attributable to general intelligence and specific personality traits rather than emotional intelligence as a construct. For example, Goleman indicated that EI accounted for 67% of the abilities deemed necessary for superior performance in leaders, and mattered twice as much as technical expertise or IQ. Other research finds that the effect of EI markers on leadership and managerial performance is non-significant when ability and personality are controlled for ,and that general intelligence correlates very closely with leadership ,Markers of EI and methods of developing it have become more widely coveted in the past decade by individuals seeking to become more effective leaders. In addition, studies have begun to provide evidence to help characterize the neural mechanisms of emotional intelligence.

In 1995, psychologist and science journalist Daniel Goleman published a book introducing most of the world to the nascent concept of emotional intelligence. The idea--that an ability to understand and manage emotions greatly increases our chances of success--quickly took off, and it went on to greatly influence the way people think about emotions and human behavior.

CHAPTER 2: Number of actions that illustrate how emotional intelligence appears in the real world.

Here are 13 of them:

1. You think about feelings.

Emotional intelligence begins with what is called self- and social awareness, the ability to recognize emotions (and their impact) in both yourself and others.

That awareness begins with reflection. You ask questions like:

What are my emotional strengths? What are my weaknesses?

How does my current mood affect my thoughts and decision making?

What's going on under the surface that influences what others say or do?

Pondering questions like these yield valuable insights that can be used to your advantage.

2. You pause.

The pause is as simple as taking a moment to stop and think before you speak or act. (Easy in theory, difficult in practice.) This can help save you from embarrassing moments or from making commitments too quickly.

In other words, pausing helps you refrain from making a permanent decision based on a temporary emotion.

3. You strive to control your thoughts.

You don't have much control over the emotion you experience in a given moment. But you can control your reaction to those emotions--by focusing on your thoughts. (As it's been said: You can't prevent a bird from landing on your head, but you can keep it from building a nest.)

By striving to control your thoughts, you resist becoming a slave to your emotions, allowing yourself to live in a way that's in harmony with your goals and values.

4. You benefit from criticism.

Nobody enjoys negative feedback. But you know that criticism is a chance to learn, even if it's not delivered in the best way. And even when it's unfounded, it gives you a window into how others think.

When you receive negative feedback, you keep your emotions in check and ask yourself: How can this make me better?

5. You show authenticity.

Authenticity doesn't mean sharing everything about yourself, to everyone, all of the time. It does mean saying what you mean, meaning what you say, and sticking to your values and principles above all else.

You know not everyone will appreciate your sharing your thoughts and feelings. But the ones who matter will.

6. You demonstrate empathy.

The ability to show empathy, which includes understanding others' thoughts and feelings, helps you connect with others. Instead of judging or labeling others, you work hard to see things through their eyes.

Empathy doesn't necessarily mean agreeing with another person's point of view. Rather, it's about striving to understand--which allows you to build deeper, more connected relationships.

7. You praise others.

All humans crave acknowledgement and appreciation. When you commend others, you satisfy that craving and build trust in the process.

This all begins when you focus on the good in others. Then, by sharing specifically what you appreciate, you inspire them to be the best version of themselves.

8. You give helpful feedback.

Negative feedback has great potential to hurt the feelings of others. Realizing this, you reframe criticism as constructive feedback, so the recipient sees it as helpful instead of harmful.

9. You apologize.

It takes strength and courage to be able to say you're sorry. But doing so demonstrates humility, a quality that will naturally draw others to you.

Emotional intelligence helps you realize that apologizing doesn't always mean you're wrong. It does mean valuing your relationship more than your ego.

10. You forgive and forget.

Hanging on to resentment is like leaving a knife inside a wound. While the offending party moves on with their life, you never give yourself the chance to heal.

When you forgive and forget, you prevent others from holding your emotions hostage--allowing you to move forward.

11. You keep your commitments.

It's common nowadays for people to break an agreement or commitment when they feel like it. Of course, bailing on an evening of Netflix with a friend will cause less harm than breaking a promise to your child or missing a major business deadline.

But when you make a habit of keeping your word--in things big and small--you develop a strong reputation for reliability and trustworthiness.

12. You help others.

One of the greatest ways to positively impact the emotions of others is to help them.

Most people don't really care where you graduated from, or even about your previous accomplishments. But what about the hours you're willing to take out of your schedule to listen or help out? Your readiness to get down in the trenches and work alongside them?

Actions like these build trust and inspire others to follow your lead when it counts.

13. You protect yourself from emotional sabotage.

You realize that emotional intelligence also has a dark side-- such as when individuals attempt to manipulate others' emotions to promote a personal agenda or for some other selfish cause.

And that's why you continue to sharpen your own emotional intelligence--to protect yourself when they do.

CHAPTER 3 : How to Improve Your Emotional Intelligence

The good news is that emotional intelligence can be learned and developed. As well as working on your skills in the five areas above, use these strategies:

Observe how you react to people. Do you rush to judgment before you know all of the facts? Do you stereotype? Look honestly at how you think and interact with other people. Try to put yourself in their place , and be more open and accepting of their perspectives and needs.

Look at your work environment. Do you seek attention for your accomplishments? Humility can be a wonderful quality, and it doesn't mean that you're shy or lack self-confidence. When you practice humility, you say that you know what you did, and you can be quietly confident about it. Give others a chance to shine – put the focus on them, and don't worry too much about getting praise for yourself.

Do a self-evaluation. Try out our emotional intelligence quiz . What are your weaknesses? Are you willing to accept that you're not perfect and that you could work on some areas to make yourself a better person? Have the courage to look at yourself honestly – it can change your life.

Examine how you react to stressful situations. Do you become upset every time there's a delay or something doesn't happen the way you want? Do you blame others or become angry at them, even when it's not their fault? The ability to stay calm and in control in difficult situations is highly valued – in the business world and outside it. Keep your emotions under control when things go wrong.

Take responsibility for your actions. If you hurt someone's feelings, apologize directly – don't ignore what you did or avoid the person.

People are usually more willing to forgive and forget if you make an honest attempt to make things right.

Examine how your actions will affect others – before you take those actions. If your decision will impact others, put yourself in their place. How will they feel if you do this? Would you want that experience? If you must take the action, how can you help others deal with the effects?

See our article on Emotional Intelligence in Leadership for specific tips related to a leadership role.

CHAPTER 4: Tips to flip your perspective and improve the relationship

One of the great perks of the workplace – the opportunity to work alongside and communicate with people from a broad range of backgrounds – can quickly become one of its biggest challenges when you have to work with someone who has a vastly different style than your own. The first and most important step in working effectively with everyone is a mindset shift – a shift to apatheia.

Apatheia, not to be confused with apathy, is a state of being where you care appropriately about what is going on around you but are not disproportionately impacted or affected by these external events. Here's how to use it to your advantage at work.

[How strong is your EQ? See our related article: Emotional intelligence test: 5 self-evaluation tools for leaders.]

The mindset sweet spot

In emotional intelligence terms, we think of apatheia as an aspect of independence. We don't want to be so emotionally close to others that they can have too much of an impact (what we call enmeshment), nor do we want to be so far away from them that we become uncaring (dissociation).

When we can find the sweet spot between these two states, we are much better able to separate what happens "out there" from impacting what happens in your head.

Dissociation might seem like a safe option, but two people who are dissociated are unlikely to be collaborative.

When you are in an enmeshed state, you may care way too much about someone else's behavior, actions, or beliefs, even when their actual impact on you is minimal. Dissociation leads to the opposite –

you do not care at all about the other person.

Dissociation might seem like a safe option when dealing with someone you don't like, but two people who are dissociated are unlikely to be collaborative. And if you are working in a team, some degree of collaboration is likely required. If you are in a leadership position, dissociation is even less of an option.

So how does this understanding of apatheia and independence help you work effectively with others? It provides a platform for the most important rule of workplace collaboration: You don't have to like the people you work with, but you do have to work with them.

Check your own emotional responses

Maybe a person who has an opposing political viewpoint to yours has said things that go strongly against your belief systems.

Perhaps the first and most important thing is to recognize that your dislike of another person boils down to the feelings you have towards them. This is a result of what you know about them as well as your experiences with them at work. Looking at it in this cold, factual way is an important step in moving toward that aforementioned sweet spot. After all, they are just a bundle of characteristics and behaviors, just like you.

Their different views on significant subjects like politics or religion can, and often do, impact how you view them. That's just human nature, and it's a tough thing to eliminate. However, you can manage your reactions to it.

For example, maybe a person who has an opposing political viewpoint to yours has said things that go strongly against your belief systems. Does that make them a bad person? No. It simply means they have a different perspective than you. Just as your perspective is a product of your experience and psychological makeup, so is theirs. If you want to have your views and perspectives respected, you must first respect theirs. This sounds easy to do, and a great many people would say they do it, but you have likely seen instances where people disrespect other people's views – it's a common occurrence.

Now that you respect their views and perspectives, can you see them as a productive, inventive, and creative team member? If they come up with an idea for a new product or a solution to a problem, can you look at that product or solution objectively, without your feelings about the person coloring your judgment?

Unfortunately, science says that is very difficult. In a bias known as reactive devaluation, we tend to place less value, or even a negative value, on ideas or proposals from people we distrust or dislike. The key here is to manage, or suspend, that distrust and dislike.

CHAPTER 5: ways to improve your one-on-one meetings

Humans crave feedback. The feedback we're given as children — from our parents, teachers, and role models — shapes how we perceive ourselves well into adulthood. And while the debate rages on regarding how different styles of feedback impact kids, a similar discussion has bubbled up in leadership circles: Does feedback work, and if so, how much is right? Is the movement toward "radical candor" helping individuals improve? Or does it create unnecessary tension, competition, and defensive behavior in the workplace? Can too much empathy be destructive to progress?

Leaders have little choice in whether or not to give feedback to their direct reports. In one-on-one discussions, individuals look to their leader to determine if they are going in the right direction and pursuing the right goals. While theories on workplace feedback will keep evolving, leaders can rely on one critical skill to make their one-on-one meetings more productive regardless of the feedback style they choose: emotional intelligence.

"Emotionally intelligent people want to know that their boss is emotionally intelligent as well," says Jonathan Feldman, CIO of the city of Asheville, NC. "That usually translates into wanting to see some self-awareness. Phrases like 'I was wrong,' 'Oh, you're right,' and 'I fell short on that one by not doing XYZ' help employees know that."

1. Always set an agenda

Uncertainty can lead to a rather big emotion: Fear.

Emotionally intelligent leaders can regulate and control their own emotions, but they know that not everyone possesses this skill. And uncertainty can lead to a rather big emotion: Fear. Be proactive in setting an agenda to quell any unnecessary fears, experts say.

"Managers need to be great at setting expectations so that the other person knows exactly what is required of them," suggests Colin D. Ellis, author of The Conscious Project Leader. This is not a skill that managers are taught, he says, but it's worth learning – before you need to have a tough unexpected conversation.

"Any meeting, even a one-on-one with a team member, can benefit from an agenda," add Drew Bird, founder at The EQ Development Group. "Even if it's just short list on a sticky note, it lets both parties know what is going to be discussed and creates some comfort about what is ahead. It's also a great way of not missing something and also managing time. Ideally, you'd collaboratively create the agenda at the beginning of the meeting so you both get an opportunity to talk about things important to you."

2. Keep progress and performance meetings separate

There's a big difference between a regular "check-in" meeting and a feedback-heavy performance discussion. Keep them totally separate, advises Bird.

"If you need to have a performance conversation, don't use a regular one-on-one progress meeting to do that. Try and make the regular one-on-one progress meetings generative, neutral spaces. If you use regular one-on-one meetings for raising a performance concern, your team member will become guarded of the regular progress meeting, as they will be unsure what's going to get discussed."

3. Start with positivity

We've all been presented with a "feedback sandwich" in our careers, and there are mixed opinions on whether it works. Tony Daniello, director of infrastructure services at Computer Design & Integration, recently told us, "If every conversation starts that way, the individual will always think there is something negative approaching whenever you give them a compliment or positive reinforcement."

Whether you sandwich or not, starting with the positives is a great way to help individuals open up, says Sanjay Malhotra, CTO of Clearbridge Mobile.

"Before jumping into a one-on-one, I like to begin with positive small talk," says Malhotra. "Something as simple as addressing a person's recent accomplishments can raise feel-good emotions that allow them to enter a positive mental state. Not only does this help to build rapport and trust with one another, but it also allows people to broaden their perceptual experience and see things in a positive light. This positivity creates an open environment where feedback is accepted and a more productive meeting is had."

4. Put your phone away

"Even these small things can add up to a big message that you don't really care about the other person."

It may seem like People Skills 101, but this lesson bears repeating: Show people that you value their time by giving them your full, undivided attention.

"Show interest and commitment to the other person by being distraction-free," says Bird. "That means no phones and no interruptions. Even a glance at your phone when it vibrates or a peek at your smartwatch sends the message that the person sitting in front of you is less important than a potential caller. You would be surprised at how even these small things can add up to a big message that you don't really care about the other person."

CHAPTER 6: Tips to apply it in everyday conversation

Are you showing emotional intelligence in work communications? Use these tips – whether you're giving feedback, seeking buy-in for an idea, or working through a misunderstanding.

Communication ranks as one of the most fundamental leadership skills. It's also the most evident manifestation of your emotional intelligence – the ability to understand and manage your own emotions and respect the emotions of others. Emotional intelligence has five characteristics, as identified by psychologist Daniel Goleman: self-awareness, self-regulation, motivation, empathy, and social skills.

Today's leaders are operating amidst tremendous volatility, change, and uncertainty: Bringing emotional intelligence to bear in your interactions with peers, bosses, partners, employees, and suppliers proves essential. Emotional intelligence can help you build stronger relationships, help others navigate challenges, and influence others in the organization.

But how can you make sure to use it in your everyday conversations?

1. Confirm your understanding

In situations when emotions are running high, it's easier to get confused or misunderstand. "It can be helpful to restate part of what you've heard," advises Hasson. You may start by saying "So am I right in thinking …" or "Can I clarify what I've heard" and then or "Can I just be clear…" before repeating back your understanding of what has been said.

"In fact, getting into a habit to listen as if you were going to repeat back (as you do when you're listening to someone give you directions) is a really good way to train yourself to focus your thoughts on listening," Hasson says.

2. Don't just listen: Watch

Pay attention to both verbal and non-verbal communication – for their interplay and any disconnects between the two. If someone says they get what you've told them but their face or shoulders say something else, follow up to find out what is going on. You might say, for example, "You said you understood, but you look unsure. Can you tell me what you're feeling about it?"

3. Frame things positively

"When things are going wrong with a piece of work, discuss what qualities and strengths [an employee or team] have that will help solve problems and contribute to overcoming difficulties".

"If you can support people and encourage them when things are difficult, you'll be inspiring them to see the best in themselves and the situation."

4. Offer more than a criticism

When you need to offer criticism, take a moment. Before you say anything, decide what, exactly, the other person has done that's a problem for you.

"You're the one with the problem. What is the solution?"

Then decide what change or improvement you want to see. "Don't just dump your criticism on the other person".

"You're the one with the problem. What is the solution?" Instead of saying something was done wrong or was not wanted, instead say, "There are a few aspects of this project I'd like you to go back over," and then explain what those things are.

5. Be more judicious with your vocabulary

"The right words make the difference" Instead of using words like "incompetent" or "wrong," you can explain that a colleague or employee "could be more careful" and then explain how. Alternatively, you can say, "It would be good if you could…" or "One thing that might help is…" to give the communication a more positive spin.

6. Avoid the blame game

Blame is a surefire way to get someone to shut down or become defensive. One way to avoid this: Start replacing "You" statements with "I" statements. Instead of saying, "You need to…" say "I'd like you to…"